# United States

## Elden Croy

John Fraser Hart and Catherine Gudis, Consultants

NATIONAL GEOGRAPHIC
WASHINGTON, D.C.

# Contents

America is one of the most diverse nations in the world. Its people come originally from all corners of the globe and represent every conceivable race and religion. From desert to ocean and mountains to plains, its geography includes some of the most pleasant and the most inhospitable places on Earth. Its urban environments range from New York City's congested cityscape with crowded sidewalks to Houston's sprawling suburbs navigable only by car.

Yet despite America's breathtaking diversity of people and places, the country is called the United States of America and employs a motto, found on all important government documents and currency: *E pluribus unum*, which is Latin for "Out of many, one." So what is it that unites this vast land?

Some say it is the American dream. Hollywood movies, television, American music, Coca-Cola, and McDonald's arches all express a belief in freedom and individualism, strength, and mobility—in short, a nation full of opportunities. This mind-set may have been inspired by the wide, open spaces as seen by early settlers from Europe, which would have appeared as a world for them to make anew. Self-creation, the powerful idea that you are not confined by your heritage but can become what you want to be through hard work and imagination, has inspired the American practices of commerce and democracy as well as its struggles for civil rights, or equality.

The achievement of luxurious, material wealth and social success are supposed to be attainable for all as well. Of course, not everyone can achieve this. Many Americans remain poor and uneducated. Still, what

seems to make the United States of America united, to hold together the diverse people, places, and experiences of this country, is the continual promise of a fresh start, the chance of improving your lot, and access to the "good life." A taste of what makes up this American dream is offered in the pages that follow.

Catherine Gudis
University of California, Riverside

▲ The promise of an
exciting life among
the skyscrapers of
Manhattan has lured
Americans to New York
City for generations.

# Many Natural Wonders

**F**OR SOME PEOPLE, MONUMENT Valley in Utah and Arizona sums up the geography of the United States. The valley is famous because it has "starred" in many Western movies. The towering outcrops, or buttes, are like nowhere else on Earth. But the spectacular valley is just one of the many different U.S. landscapes. The country is the third largest in the world and contains a wide variety of scenery, from snow-covered mountains and dry deserts to steamy swamps and huge lakes. Although the United States has some of the largest cities on Earth, there are entire regions that are too cold or too dry for many people to live. As the writer Gertrude Stein said: "In the United States there is more space where nobody is than where anybody is."

◀ **Monument Valley was sculpted over millions of years by wind and rain. The towering "thumbs" of two of these buttes have earned them the name the Mittens.**

# WHAT'S THE WEATHER LIKE?

The United States is so big, it is difficult to describe the weather. It varies from the subtropical climate of the South to the deserts of the Southwest and the freezing winters of the Midwest. In the Pacific Northwest it often rains, while the middle of the country has hot summers and cold winters. The map opposite shows the physical features of the United States. Labels on this map and on similar maps throughout this book identify places pictured in each chapter.

## MAP KEY

Polar
Subarctic
Tundra
Tropical
Dry
Tropical wet & dry
Arid
Semiarid
Mild
Mediterranean
Humid subtropical
Marine west coast
Continental
Cool Summer
Warm Summer
Highland

Bering Sea
Gulf of Alaska
0 400 mi
0 400 km

Pacific Ocean
0 200 mi
0 200 km

Rocky Mountains
Appalachian Mountains
Gulf of Mexico
Pacific Ocean
Atlantic Ocean
0 mi 500
0 km 500

# Fast Facts

**OFFICIAL NAME:** United States of America

**TYPE OF GOVERNMENT:** Federal republic

**CAPITAL:** Washington, D.C.

**POPULATION:** 303,824,640

**OFFICIAL LANGUAGE:** None

**MONETARY UNIT:** Dollar

**AREA:** 3,718,712 square miles (9,826,630 sq km)

**BORDERS:** Canada, Mexico

**HIGHEST POINT:** Mount McKinley, 20,320 feet (6,194 m)

**LOWEST POINT:** Death Valley, −282 feet (−86 m)

**MAJOR MOUNTAIN RANGES:** Alaska Range, Appalachian Mountains, Cascade Range, Rocky Mountains, Sierra Nevada

**MAJOR RIVERS:** Arkansas, Colorado, Columbia, Snake, Mississippi, Missouri, Ohio, Rio Grande, and St. Lawrence

# Average Temperature & Rainfall

Average High/Low Temperatures; Yearly Rainfall

**NEW YORK CITY, NEW YORK:** 62° F (17° C) / 47° F (8° C); 44 in (113 cm)

**MIAMI, FLORIDA:** 76° F (24° C) / 50° F (10° C); 14 in (35 cm)

**CHICAGO, ILLINOIS:** 59° F (15° C) / 42° F (5° C); 36 in (92 cm)

**EL PASO, TEXAS:** 77° F (25° C) / 49° F (9° C); 9 in (22 cm)

**DENVER, COLORADO:** 64° F (18° C) / 36° F (2° C); 15 in (39 cm)

**SEATTLE, WASHINGTON:** 60° F (15° C) / 46° F (8° C); 36 in (93 cm)

**LOS ANGELES, CALIFORNIA:** 74° F (23° C) / 54° F (12° C); 12 in (31 cm)

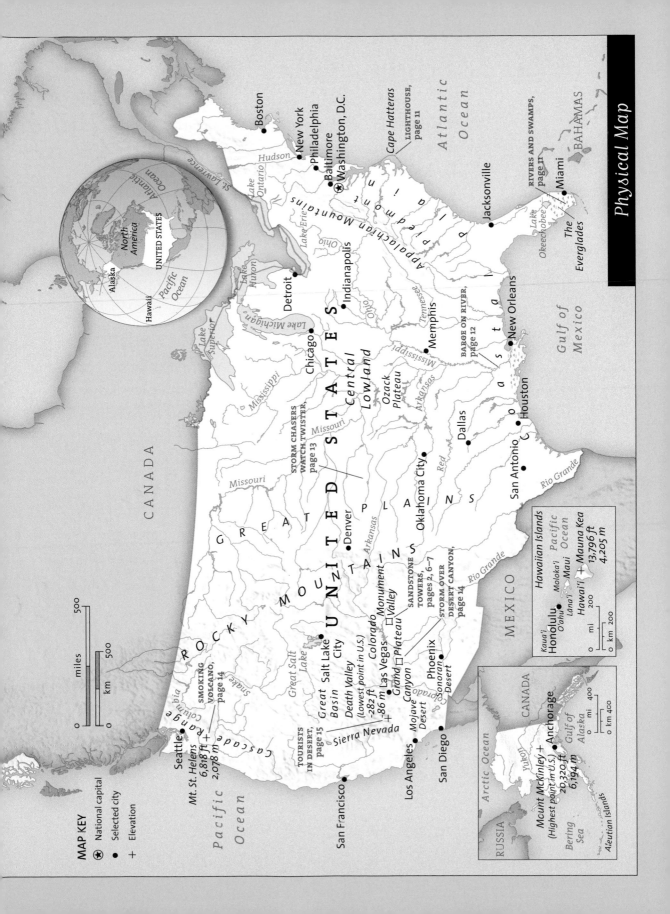

MAP KEY

⊛ National capital
• Selected city
+ Elevation

CANADA

Pacific Ocean

Atlantic Ocean

North America

UNITED STATES

Alaska

Hawaii

Pacific Ocean

Atlantic Ocean

Hudson

St. Lawrence

Lake Ontario

Lake Erie

Boston

New York

Philadelphia

Baltimore

Washington, D.C.

Cape Hatteras

LIGHTHOUSE, page 11

Atlantic Ocean

Jacksonville

RIVERS AND SWAMPS, page 11

Miami

BAHAMAS

Lake Okeechobee

The Everglades

Gulf of Mexico

New Orleans

Appalachian Mountains

Piedmont

Ohio

Lake Huron

Lake Michigan

Detroit

Indianapolis

Chicago

Lake Superior

Mississippi

Central Lowland

Ozark Plateau

Tennessee

Memphis

Mississippi

Arkansas

BARGE ON RIVER, page 12

Houston

C o a s t a l   P l a i n

Dallas

Red

San Antonio

Rio Grande

Missouri

STORM CHASERS WATCH TWISTER, page 13

Missouri

G R E A T   P L A I N S

Denver

Oklahoma City

Arkansas

Rio Grande

MEXICO

U N I T E D   S T A T E S

G R E A T

R O C K Y   M O U N T A I N S

Columbia

Cascade Range

Seattle

Mt. St. Helens 6,818 ft + 2,078 m

SMOKING VOLCANO, page 15

Snake

Great Salt Lake

Salt Lake City

Death Valley (Lowest point in U.S.) -282 ft -86 m

Las Vegas

Sierra Nevada

TOURISTS IN DESERT, page 15

San Francisco

Los Angeles

Mojave Desert

San Diego

Colorado

Monument Valley

Colorado Plateau

Grand Canyon

SANDSTONE TOWERS, pages 2, 6–7

Phoenix

Sonoran Desert

STORM OVER DESERT CANYON, page 14

Pacific Ocean

miles

km

500

500

0

Hawaiian Islands

Pacific Ocean

Kaua'i
Honolulu
O'ahu   Moloka'i
Lana'i   Maui
Hawai'i + Mauna Kea 13,796 ft 4,205 m

mi   200
km   200

0

CANADA

RUSSIA

Arctic Ocean

Yukon

Mount McKinley + 20,320 ft (Highest point in U.S.) 6,194 m

Anchorage

Bering Sea

Gulf of Alaska

Aleutian Islands

mi   400
km   400

0

# Beautiful Land

The song *America the Beautiful*, written by Katharine Lee Bates in 1893, celebrates the diversity of land that stretches "from sea to shining sea." The two "seas" are actually the Atlantic and Pacific Oceans, which form the country's eastern and western edges. To the north the United States is bordered by Canada and to the south by Mexico. The main part of the country, containing 48 states, is known as the contiguous United States, sometimes called the Lower Forty-Eight. The remaining two states are Alaska, the largest state, located in the far northwest of the North American continent, and Hawaii, a group of islands in the Pacific Ocean—2,100 miles (3,400 km) west of California.

▲ Mount McKinley, the highest point in North America, rises above the meadows and forest of Denali National Park in Alaska.

# In the East

Geographers divide the United States into regions based on their landscapes and climate. The first region is the Atlantic Plain that runs along the eastern seaboard. The country's oldest cities are located on the east coast, including Boston, New York City, Philadelphia, and Washington, D.C. The coast is

# RIVER OF GRASS

At the southern tip of Florida is a wetland with an unusual name: the Everglades. No one knows how the Everglades got its name, but some suggest that it comes from the "River Glades." The Native Americans called the region *Pa-Hay-Okee*, which means "grassy water."

Sawgrass grows in the shallow water that flows from Lake Okeechobee in a slow-moving river 50 miles (80 km) wide and 100 miles (160 km) long—but rarely more than a foot deep. The Everglades (above) end in mangrove swamps that border the Gulf of Mexico and Florida Bay. Rare animals found in the swampy waters include the American crocodile, the Florida panther (a type of puma), the West Indian manatee, and several species of sea turtles.

indented with estuaries that provide natural harbors. The weather is colder and more extreme in New England at the northern end of the plain. In the far south, the peninsula of Florida has a subtropical climate.

To the west, the Atlantic Plain is divided from the heart of the country by the Appalachian Mountains, which run from Maine to Alabama. The Appalachians are so old that they have largely eroded away. The highest summit is only half the height of many peaks in the Rockies, a much younger range in the West.

The lighthouse at Cape Hatteras in North Carolina is the only tall building seen for miles along the flat, sandy East Coast.

# The Heart of the Country

The west side of the Appalachians is known by Americans as the Middle West, or simply the Midwest. Most of it is covered by a large, flat grassland known as the prairie, which is French for "meadow." Tall grass once covered more than 140 million acres (57 million hectares) of North America, but much of the Midwest has been plowed up into fields. Today, only 4 percent of the original prairie remains.

To the north, five huge bodies of fresh water called the Great Lakes overlap the Canadian border. Only Lake Michigan lies entirely in the United States. To the south is the low-lying coast of the Gulf of Mexico, where the Mississippi River meets the sea. The Mississippi, together with its tributary, the Missouri, forms one of the largest river systems in the world. It flows south through the Midwest, draining more than 40 percent of the Lower Forty-Eight states. The river collects huge amounts of sediment. When it reaches the Gulf, the silt settles and makes a network of mud islands. The river splits into hundreds of channels to create the Mississippi Delta.

West of the Mississippi lie the Great Plains. This drier region has shorter grasses than the prairies. In the late 19th century, this area represented the frontier of U.S. settlement: It became famous as the Wild West. In the 1930s, drought turned much of the soil of the southern plains into dust. Crops spoiled and huge clouds of dust swept what became known as the "Dust Bowl."

## Natural Hazards

Drought and dust storms are not the only natural threats to the United States. The southern Midwest is swept by hundreds of tornadoes each year, while the Gulf of Mexico and East Coast are regularly struck by hurricanes. Farther west, there are active volcanoes in

## CHASING TORNADOES

The central United States has more tornadoes than anywhere else in the world—about 800 a year. Great masses of air from the Pacific Ocean, the Gulf of Mexico, the Arctic Ocean, and the Atlantic Ocean crash into each other over the Great Plains, creating columns of air that spin at up to 200 miles (320 km) per hour in a tornado. Most of them form in Tornado Alley, a strip of land that runs between the Rockies and Appalachian Mountains. Homes here have basement shelters, and towns sound sirens when tornadoes are approaching. For most, the sirens are a signal to head for shelter—but for a small number of enthusiasts, it is a call to grab a camera and head straight toward a tornado. Many are scientists who want to figure out how dangerous tornadoes form in the hope that they can predict them. Others are storm chasers (below) who just want to see the twisters up close.

▲ The rocks at the bottom of the Grand Canyon are 1.8 billion years old.

Alaska and the Pacific Northwest, California, and Hawaii. California also lies on the boundary between two plates of Earth's crust: the San Andreas fault. The fault has caused severe earthquakes in San Francisco and Los Angeles when the plates rub against one another.

## DISASTER AND RECOVERY

For centuries, Mount St. Helens was just one of the many dormant volcanoes at the north end of the Cascade Range in Washington. Then on May 18, 1980, a huge blast blew away the top 1,200 feet (366 m) of the volcano leaving a smoking crater (below). A mass of rock rushed down the mountain, burying homes, roads, and lakes: 57 people died. Ash from the explosion fell in 11 states. The explosion knocked down all the trees and the thick gray ash killed all the plants. But within months green shoots reappeared, and a year after the disaster, footprints showed that deer were back on the mountain.

## Rugged West

Beyond the Plains, mountains and plateaus cover the remaining third of the United States. The Rocky Mountains, Sierra Nevada, and Cascade Range are known as the Western Cordillera.

The West is home to yet more unusual landscapes. One of the

## LOWEST OF THE LOW

The floor of Death Valley in California is the lowest point in the Western Hemisphere. Badwater Basin is 282 feet (85.5 m) below sea level and is covered in salt flats (right) and sand dunes. Only 2 inches (5 cm) of rain falls here each year. The valley is sheltered from cold and rain by the steep mountains on either side, which makes it one of the hottest places on Earth. The temperature often reaches 120° F (49° C).

most famous is the Grand Canyon, a 277-mile (446-km) gorge in the Arizona Desert cut a mile (1.6 km) deep by the Colorado River.

The lowland plain of the West Coast is much narrower than in the east. In many places the coastal mountains plunge right into the ocean. This creates some of the country's most spectacular coastlines, such as California's Big Sur.

The coast also has sheltered bays that provide natural harbors. Seattle and San Diego both grew around bays, but the San Francisco harbor is the largest in the world. Another West Coast city, Los Angeles, grew for other reasons. In the 1920s, oil was found in the area, which caused an influx of people. Meanwhile, movie studios also moved from New York to the city's Hollywood district. They came to take advantage of the balmy Californian climate, which had enough sunshine to allow outdoor filming throughout the year.

# National Treasures

**S**WOOPING OVER THE WATER, the magnificent bald eagle prepares to grab a fish. The bird is the symbol of the United States. In 1782, Thomas Jefferson and the other Founders chose the bald eagle to express their majestic vision of the new country. Not everyone agreed with the decision. Benjamin Franklin said that the eagle was "a bird of bad moral character." He wanted to choose the turkey, because it was a "bird of courage."

With a wingspan of up to 96 inches (234 cm), the bald eagle can weigh more than 15 pounds (7 kg) and can kill young deer. Despite its name, the bald eagle is not bald at all. Its head and tail are covered in thick white feathers, while the rest of the body is brown. The eagle's name comes from the old-fashioned English word *ballede*, which means "white."

◀ Bald eagles live in nearly every U.S. state, but most are found in Alaska.

# PROTECTING NATURE

In 1872, President Ulysses S. Grant signed a bill that made history. He created the world's first national park, Yellowstone National Park in Wyoming, although Abraham Lincoln first suggested the idea of preserving America's wilderness for all to enjoy. On July 1, 1864, Lincoln, in the midst of the Civil War, took time to sign a bill granting Yosemite National Park and its magnificent trees to the state of California, "for the benefit of the people, for their resort and recreation, to hold them inalienable for all time." Today, Yosemite and 46 other parks are managed by the National Park Service, created in 1916 by President Woodrow Wilson. More than 80 million acres (323,749 sq. km) of land are in national parks, including Arizona's Grand Canyon, Mesa Verde in Colorado, and the Statue of Liberty in New York City. The map below shows the vegetation zones—or what grows where—in the United States of America.

▲ **Tourists walk through a tunnel cut in the trunk of a giant sequoia in Yosemite National Park, California.**

## Species at Risk

The United States has made great progress in reversing the fate of a number of endangered species, including the bald eagle and California condor. Penalties for harming threatened species are strictly enforced and with the help of education programs, people are more aware of the need to protect indigenous species. Species at risk include:

- American crocodile
- Big long-nosed bat
- Black-footed ferret
- Giant kangaroo rat
- Hawaiian monk seal
- Lesser prairie chicken
- Antelope squirrel
- Polar bear
- Red wolf
- Sea otter
- Steller sea lion
- Yellownose snake

# Vegetation & Ecosystems Map

**Oceans, seas, and labels:**

Pacific Ocean

Atlantic Ocean

Gulf of Mexico

Arctic Ocean

Bering Sea

Gulf of Alaska

**Countries/regions:**

CANADA

MEXICO

RUSSIA

**Cities:**

Boston

New York

Philadelphia

Washington, D.C.

Miami

New Orleans

Dallas

Detroit

Chicago

Indianapolis

Denver

Phoenix

Los Angeles

San Diego

San Francisco

Seattle

Honolulu

Anchorage

**Physical features:**

St. Lawrence

Lake Ontario

Lake Erie

Lake Huron

Lake Michigan

Lake Superior

Ohio

Mississippi

Missouri

Arkansas

Red

Rio Grande

Colorado

Snake

Columbia

Yukon

Appalachian Mountains

ROCKY MOUNTAINS

GREAT PLAINS

Cascade Range

Sierra Nevada

Great Basin

Great Salt Lake

Mojave Desert

Sonoran Desert

Hawaiian Islands

Aleutian Islands

Kaua'i

O'ahu

Moloka'i

Lāna'i

Maui

Hawai'i

PACIFIC OCEAN

**National Parks and labels:**

Glacier N.P.

Yellowstone N.P.

Mesa Verde N.P.

Arches N.P.

Bryce Canyon N.P.

Zion N.P.

Death Valley N.P.

Grand Canyon N.P.

Yosemite N.P.

Great Smoky Mountains N.P.

Everglades NP

Wrangell-St. Elias N.P.

Gates of the Arctic N.P.

Denali N.P.

Katmai N.P.

**Photo/page callouts:**

PRONGHORNS RUNNING IN THE ROAD, page 25

FLYING GOOSE, page 22

HERD OF BISON, page 24

RATTLESNAKE TRAPPERS, page 24

BABY ALLIGATOR, page 22

MANATEE UNDERWATER, page 21

SEAWEED UNDERWATER, page 20 SEA OTTER, page 21

DRY FOREST, page 23

TOURISTS WALK UNDER TREE TRUNK, page 18

SWOOPING EAGLE, pages 2, 16–17

## MAP KEY

**Primary Vegetation Zones / Ecosystems**

Boreal forest

Deserts and dry shrublands

Flooded grasslands

Mediterranean scrub

Temperate broadleaf and mixed forests

Temperate coniferous forests

Temperate grasslands

Tropical and subtropical broadleaf forests

Tropical and subtropical grasslands

Tundra

**Protected Lands**

Selected national parks

**Scale bars:**

miles

0  500

km  0  500

mi  0  200

km  0  200

mi  0  400

km  0  400

# Home of Variety

The United States is one of the most ecologically diverse countries on Earth. It is home to about 2,000 species of mammals, and thousands more species of reptiles, amphibians, and birds. Due in part to a 100-year history of conservation programs, many species that were once endangered are now flourishing. Animals that have benefited from such programs include gray wolves, golden eagles, prairie dogs, and bison.

# On the Waterfront

The United States has ocean to the west, east, and south. The Pacific coast is foggy and damp in the north and hot and dry in the south. The cold coastal waters off northern California are home to vast underwater forests of seaweed called kelp. The forests create a natural barrier that protects the shoreline from large waves. Californian sea lions seek shelter among the kelp to hide from great white sharks that patrol farther off shore.

Sea otters also live in the kelp. They collect shellfish from the seabed and love to eat sea urchins. The urchins eat kelp roots, so without the otters, the forests would die. About a century ago, fur trappers

▲ The giant kelp that makes up California's kelp forests is the fastest growing plant on Earth. In warm conditions it can grow 2 feet (60 cm) in just one day.

had reduced California's sea otter population to a few dozen. The kelp forests declined, and as a result storm waves began to erode the California coast faster than usual. Now sea otters are heavily protected.

Along the eastern seaboard, the Atlantic Ocean stretches from the lobster-filled waters of Maine in the north to the warm waters of Florida. Seagrass that grows in Florida's calm inlets is eaten by manatees. These sea mammals look like a cross between a cow and seal—but are actually related to elephants.

Florida is also home to the endangered American crocodile, which lives in freshwater lakes but also swims in coastal seas. The American alligator only lives in freshwater and is much more common. Alligators kill about three people a year in the United States. Any

# MISSISSIPPI FLYWAY

In fall, the skies above the Mississippi Valley are full of large flocks of birds flying south. This is the longest bird migration of the Western Hemisphere. The birds are flying from the cold north en route to their winter homes. The 3,000-mile flight (4,800 km) from the mouth of the Mackenzie River in Canada to the Mississippi Delta is quite an easy journey for the birds. There are no mountain ranges to cross along the entire route, and the rivers give the birds plenty of food and water as they fly south. When the birds reach the Gulf Coast, they spread out and head in different directions.

▲ Many of the birds flying down the Mississippi are waterfowl, such as these Canada geese.

gator longer than 6.5 feet (2 m) can kill a human. Most casualties are children playing beside water, but attacks are actually pretty rare.

## On the Timberline

The ancient woodlands that once covered the eastern and southern portions of the United States have, for the most part, been cleared. However, huge areas of forest remain elsewhere in the country, especially in the mountains of the West. One of the most unusual is the Olympic National Forest in the northwest corner of Washington State. It is a rain forest: nearly 10 feet (3.5 m) of rain falls there each year. This rain forest is not like the hot and steamy jungle of tropical rain forests. It is a temperate forest,

▶ A baby alligator takes a ride on its mother's head in Florida's Everglades.

meaning it has moderate temperatures. However, vegetation grows just as quickly as in the tropics, despite the colder weather. Every surface is covered in plantlife, from huge conifer trees to lush mosses.

## Staying Dry

The United States has three different types of deserts—all of them in the West. The Great Basin Desert, centered in Nevada and Utah, is a cold and high place. When winter snow melts in spring it provides enough water for slow-growing pines and shrubs to make it through the rest of the year. The second desert is the Sonoran, which extends from Arizona and southern California into northern Mexico. It is the most biologically diverse desert in the world. It is watered by summer and winter rains, which support

## TAKING ITS TIME

The Earth's oldest living inhabitant is a tree. To be precise, it is a Great Basin bristlecone pine called "Methuselah." Methuselah is almost 5,000 years old and is named after a person from the Bible who supposedly lived until he was 969. Methuselah and other bristlecone pines live in dry mountains. They may survive for centuries, but they grow very slowly and only reach about 50 feet (15 m) tall.

▲ The location of Methuselah in the Inyo National Forest is kept secret in order to protect it.

fast-growing flowers that bloom in spring, as well as other slower-growing woody plants.

The third U.S. desert is the Mojave. It is home to the Joshua tree, a member of the yucca family that is native to the Southwest. One of the few animals to survive in the Mojave's extreme heat is the gila monster, one of only two venomous lizards in the world. Another deadly reptile found in the desert is the western diamondback snake, the largest type of rattlesnake in North America.

▲ American bison—or buffalo—graze in Custer State Park in South Dakota. Bison are the largest herbivores living in North America.

▼ Every year thousands of rattlesnakes are captured in "round-ups." Some are put on display at public shows, while most are killed to make snakeskin items.

## The Plains and Mountains

The cougar is the largest cat in the United States. It is most common in the western mountains and among the chaparral, thick shrubs that cover the dry hills and

## IN THE FAST LANE

The one truly unique American mammal is the pronghorn, which lives on the prairie and is the "antelope" mentioned in the song *Home on the Range.* However, antelopes do not live in North America. Although they might look similar, pronghorns are neither deer nor relatives of goats or cattle. Instead they are the last survivors of a group of plant-eating mammals called the Antilocapridae. Like antelopes, pronghorns have horns, with a single branch, or prong. Also like an antelope, the pronghorn's head gear is made of bone and stays on for life. However, the soft covering of the horns falls off each year and then grows back—in the same way deer regrow antlers.

Pronghorns graze on the prairie and gather in herds of several hundred animals in the winter. They are built for running from danger and can reach speeds of 60 miles (95 km) an hour! And they can spring nearly 20 feet (6 m) forward in a single bound.

▲ Pronghorns sometimes run alongside cars on remote roads.

plateaus. The cats prey on bighorn sheep and deer that try to stay safe by grazing on steep cliffs or by hiding in the alpine forests.

On the plains, animals have other ways of protecting themselves. Bison are large enough to evade most enemies, except for one. Once, millions of bison grazed on the plains. Native Americans hunted bison for food and used the skin and bones to make clothes and tools. European settlers killed off almost all the bison for their hide, bringing them close to extinction. Today, nearly all bison live in herds raised in captivity.

# Land of the Free

**A** CRACKED OLD BELL LIES AT THE heart of American history. The Liberty Bell is said to have been rung in 1776 to mark the first reading of the Declaration of Independence. The document expressed the decision of Americans to create their own country: the United States of America. The bell hung in Independence Hall in Philadelphia. It was rung again when the U.S. Constitution was signed there in 1787. In 1800, Washington, D.C. replaced Philadelphia as the nation's capital, but the Liberty Bell remained in Philadelphia. It was rung each year on the Fourth of July and to celebrate the birthday of George Washington, the first U.S. president. However, in 1846, the bell's crack got so bad that it stopped working. Today it is just given a light tap each year.

◀ Schoolchildren get close enough to the Liberty Bell to read the inscription around the top: "Proclaim liberty throughout all the land unto all the inhabitants thereof."

# THE FIRST AMERICANS

About 15,000 years ago, during the last ice age, sea levels fell and exposed a land bridge across the Bering Strait, the stretch of water that now separates Russia from Alaska. For the first time, people could walk to America from northern Asia. The people that did are the ancestors of today's Native Americans.

Early Americans were hunter-gatherers, surviving by eating only what they could catch and find. They did not grow food or keep animals or wear clothes made from animal skins. However, they did invent some simple technology. Near Clovis, New Mexico, archaeologists found stone tools used by people that lived there around 13,000 B.C.

▲ Early Americans hunted woolly mammoths using wood and stone weapons. Mammoths became extinct about 4,000 years ago.

## Time line

This chart shows some of the important dates in the history of the United States from native cultures to the present.

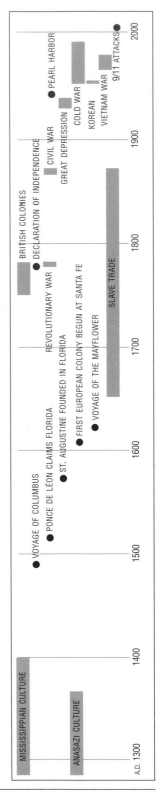

A.D. 1300
1400
1500
1600
1700
1800
1900
2000

MISSISSIPPIAN CULTURE

ANASAZI CULTURE

VOYAGE OF COLUMBUS

PONCE DE LÉON CLAIMS FLORIDA

ST. AUGUSTINE FOUNDED IN FLORIDA

FIRST EUROPEAN COLONY BEGUN AT SANTA FE

VOYAGE OF THE MAYFLOWER

SLAVE TRADE

BRITISH COLONIES

DECLARATION OF INDEPENDENCE

REVOLUTIONARY WAR

CIVIL WAR

GREAT DEPRESSION

COLD WAR

KOREAN WAR

VIETNAM WAR

PEARL HARBOR

9/11 ATTACKS

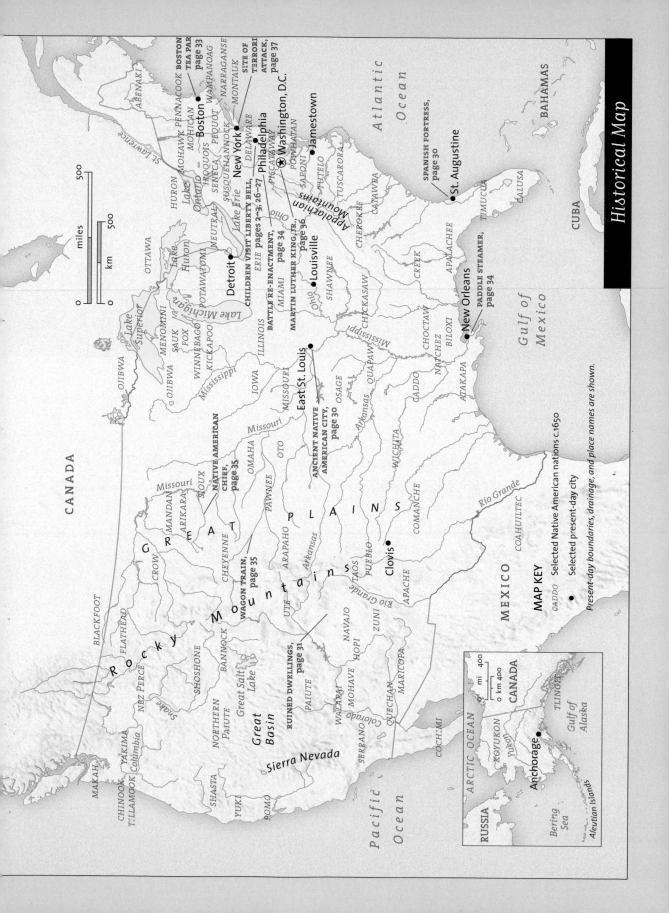

▲ This painting recreates the ancient city of Cahokia located a few miles northeast of modern-day St. Louis.

▼ Dating from 1672, the Castillo de San Marcos at St. Augustine, Florida, is the oldest stone building made by European settlers.

# Before Columbus

When Europeans arrived in the Americas in the late 15th century, many native cultures already lived there. More than 200 different languages were spoken in North America alone. The Mississippians, who lived at Cahokia in present-day Illinois between A.D. 700 and 1400, built large mounds to bury their dead. At its peak around 900 years ago, Cahokia was home to as many as 20,000 people.

# Enter the Europeans

American history changed forever in 1492, when an Italian sailor working for the Spanish royal family arrived in the Caribbean. Christopher Columbus was looking for a new sea route to China by sailing west from Europe. Instead, he stumbled upon a "New World."

The Spanish took the lead in exploring. In 1513, they claimed Florida, which later became home to the first permanent European settlement in North America: St. Augustine. The French set up colonies around the Great Lakes, while an English colony started at Jamestown, Virginia, in 1607. Soon the Dutch and Swedish also settled on the East Coast.

In 1620, 102 Englishmen and women, known as the first pilgrims, crossed the Atlantic on the *Mayflower*. Many hoped to find freedom to practice their form of Christianity. They settled in what is now Massachusetts but found it difficult to grow food. They would have

## DISAPPEARING CLIFF DWELLERS

One of the most sophisticated of all the early American cultures was the Anasazi. This was the name given to the Pueblo people who lived on the Colorado Plateau, where Utah, Colorado, Arizona, and New Mexico meet today—known as the Four Corners. We know about the Anasazi from their beautiful pottery and the adobe houses they lived in. Many Anasazi dwellings are built on cliffs or in canyons, which made them secure from attack. The Pueblo Bonito village in Chaco Canyon, New Mexico, had several hundred rooms (right).

The Anasazi disappeared in the 14th century. It is likely that the Four Corners became much drier during that time, making it hard to grow enough food.

starved if not for the kindness of native people. The pilgrims' first successful harvest is still celebrated by American families today at Thanksgiving.

Many Europeans were eager to move to the new colonies. But other newcomers had no choice. During the 17th century, slave traders shipped Africans to North America. There were 1,600 slaves in America by 1650; a century later, the figure was 236,420—about 20 percent of the total population at that time.

▲ A replica of the *Mayflower* recreates the voyage of the pilgrims that occured in 1620.

▶ Slaves were brought to America in shackles. Even the children wore small irons (bottom).

# Revolution!

By the start of the 18th century, the British had taken over the Swedish and Dutch colonies on the East Coast. The French had trading posts along the Mississippi River. They founded the city of New Orleans near the river's delta in 1718. In the 1750s France and Britain began to fight in the Ohio Valley and Great Lakes. Britain won the war, and France gave up all of its lands east of the Mississippi in 1763. The British king, George III, wanted the Americans to pay for the war with France and raised taxes. The colonists were outraged that they did not have the right to protest the tax hikes in the British parliament. In April 1775, fighting broke out between colonial militia and British troops. The Revolutionary War had begun. The patriots, as the rebel colonists became known, set out to change British laws. But many came to believe that they could only protect their freedom by creating their own country. In the summer of 1776, representatives of the Thirteen Colonies met at Philadelphia. On July 4, the Declaration of Independence was signed after being drafted by Thomas Jefferson. With help from the French, the Americans finally defeated the British in 1783. The United States of America was born. George Washington, who had commanded the Continental Army, became the first president.

▲ History enthusiasts recreate the 1773 Boston Tea Party, in which protesters, dressed as Native Americans, threw tea into the harbor to rebel against British taxes.

## Early Troubles

By 1800, the population of the United States had grown to five million whites and one million African slaves. Many Americans believed that slavery was wrong. By the 1830s, it was illegal in the northern states. In the South, however, people wanted to keep slavery. The economy relied on crops like cotton, which needed a lot of workers to grow and harvest.

By 1860, tensions over slavery were escalating. The number of states had grown to 37 as the United States

# TAXATION WITHOUT REPRESENTATION

One of the slogans that rallied Americans to rebel against the British was, "No taxation without representation!" The colonists paid taxes to the king but had no politicians working for them in Britain. Ironically, people living in Washington, D.C., the U.S. capital, are fighting a similar battle today. The people of D.C. (District of Colombia) are not fully represented in Congress, the government that works in the city. A delegate represents the city, but he or she cannot vote on new laws. But nevertheless, the people living in the capital city are still expected to pay their taxes!

## STEAM POWER!

In the early days of the United States, rivers were the only highways through the country. The Ohio River carried sailboats and barges west, and the Mississippi took them south. Sailing upstream could be difficult, however, until the arrival of the steamboat. In 1787, John Fitch tested a boat powered by steam on the Delaware River. In 1807, Robert Fulton invented a paddle steamer. His boat could travel up the Hudson River from New York City to Albany in just five days. Steamboats revolutionized travel and brought new settlers to the West. In 1816, it took three and a half weeks to travel from New Orleans, Louisiana, to Louisville, Kentucky. By 1853, the same journey only took less than five days.

▲ Steamboats today are used to take tourists on cruises up and down the Mississippi River.

▼ Military historians reenact the Battle of Gettysburg of 1863. It was the bloodiest battle in U.S. history—151,000 Americans fought on both sides and after three days of fighting, 8,000 of them had died.

continued to expand west. When Abraham Lincoln took office in 1861, he opposed slavery in any new state but allowed it to continue where it already existed. Despite this, some states disagreed with Lincoln's decision. In all, eleven southern slave states quit the Union and formed the Confederate States of America. Lincoln went to war to hold the Union together. Americans took sides: whole families were divided by the Civil War. Four years of fighting cost 600,000 lives before the North won. The Union was preserved—and slavery ended throughout the country.

# A Mighty Nation Emerges

When the Civil War ended, the U.S. had a lot to figure out. Over the next decade the young country underwent a period of reconstruction, implementing new laws and re-connecting the divided nation. It was not long until the country was once again thriving as an influx of immigrants arrived seeking new opportunities. Many headed west to look for land and came into conflict with Native Americans. The U.S. Army forced groups onto reservations—land set aside by the government.

In the early 20th century, industry grew rapidly. The Ford Motor Company in Detroit made cars that even ordinary people could afford. However, the stock market crashed in 1929, and the Great Depression began. By 1932, one in four Americans had no job.

The United States was still recovering from the Depression when the U.S. naval base at Pearl Harbor, Hawaii, was attacked by Japanese aircraft in 1941. The United States entered World War II and was on the winning side four years later. The United States

▲ Arvol Looking Horse, the Sioux chief for more than last 40 years, performs a ritual at the reservation in South Dakota, where the Sioux have lived since 1876.

## GO WEST, YOUNG MAN!

Between the 1840s and 1870s, millions of Americans sought a new life in the West. For many people the journey began beside the Mississippi near St. Louis. Belongings were transferred from steamboats to covered wagons (right), and groups set off in lines, known as wagon "trains." The trains followed trails to California, Oregon, and the Southwest, taking months to reach their destination. In the 1870s, the wagons were replaced by railcars when railroads were built between the East and West Coasts.

emerged as a world superpower. The communist Soviet Union was equally powerful, and the two nations became locked in a struggle for political influence, known as the Cold War. This conflict led to several wars in foreign countries, and many thousands of U.S. soldiers fought in the Korean War (1950–1953) and the Vietnam War (1961–1975).

▲ Martin Luther King, Jr. gathers with other civil rights leaders in Washington, D.C. in 1963 during the March on Washington—the largest political protest in U.S. history. A few hours later, King set out his vision for the United States in his "I have a dream" speech.

## Cracks Appear

At home the United States was changing dramatically. Since the Civil War, black and white Americans in the South had lived in separate communities. African Americans went to different schools and even had to sit in the back of a bus. In 1954, the Supreme Court declared that this segregation was illegal. African Americans began a long struggle for equal civil rights. They were led by the preacher Martin Luther King, Jr. He was assassinated in 1968, but the civil rights movement went on. Although the struggle for racial equality continues even today a major landmark was reached in 2008 when Americans elected Barack Obama as the first African-American president.

## The New Century

The Cold War ended in 1991 when the Soviet Union broke up. The United States became the world's only

# FLY THEM TO THE MOON

**W**hen the Soviet Union launched the satellite *Sputnik I* into orbit in 1957, a space race began between the Soviets and the United States. In 1961, after the first missions by the U.S. National Aeronautics and Space Administration (NASA), President John F. Kennedy started the Apollo Program to send people to the moon. On July 21, 1969, Neil Armstrong became the first human to walk on the moon. In total, 12 Americans visited the Moon—so far no other country has sent a crew.

▲ Astronaut James Irwin salutes during the Apollo 15 mission in July 1971 beside the lunar module and rover, or "moon buggy."

superpower. But it still had enemies. On September 11, 2001, Islamist terrorists attacked New York and Washington, D.C. Although some Americans were reluctant to support military action, the United States fought back, going to war in Afghanistan in October 2001 and invading Iraq in 2003.

▼ Smoke rises from the remains of the World Trade Center in lower Manhattan following the terrorist attacks of September 11, 2001.

# A Nation
## of
# Settlers

**W**ALK THROUGH THE STREETS of Chinatown in San Francisco, California, and you might think you were in Hong Kong or Beijing. This part of the city is home to the largest Chinese community outside of Asia. It is also home to many Southeast Asians, including Vietnamese, Laotians, Koreans, and Thais.

Only about 1 percent of U.S. citizens are Native Americans. The other 99 percent are descended from different ethnic groups that have settled in the country over the last 500 years. For example, many Chinese-Americans are relatives of the people who arrived in California in the 1840s to work on the railroads that were being built across the country. More arrived during the California Gold Rush of 1849.

◀ A cable car rolls through the intersection of Grant Avenue and California Street in San Francisco's Chinatown.

# TOWN AND COUNTRY

The United States is an urban country, but it wasn't always this way. One hundred years ago, most Americans lived in the countryside. During the 20th century, job opportunities drove millions to cities, which quickly became crowded. By the 1950s, people began to move to suburbs on the edge of the cities so they could have houses and yards but still be close to work. Americans are the most mobile people on Earth. The average American moves as many as 12 times in his or her lifetime. The 21st century saw the start of another population shift with more Americans moving to remote areas again. Telecommunication allows them to work from anywhere.

▼ A mother and son carry their groceries home in the quiet town of Charleston, South Carolina.

# Common American Words

There is no official language in the United States but almost everyone understands English, even if they speak another language at home. American English has many words taken from the other languages spoken by early settlers:

| | |
|---|---|
| cookie, stoop, bum | Dutch |
| rodeo, barbecue, mesa | Spanish |
| levee, prairie, butte | French |
| opossum, raccoon, squash | Native American |
| scram, kindergarten, hamburger | German |

| 1950 / 158 million | 1970 / 210 million |
|---|---|
| 64% urban / 36% rural | 74% urban / 26% rural |
| **1990 / 256 million** | **2005 / 298 million** |
| 75% urban / 25% rural | 81% urban / 19% rural |

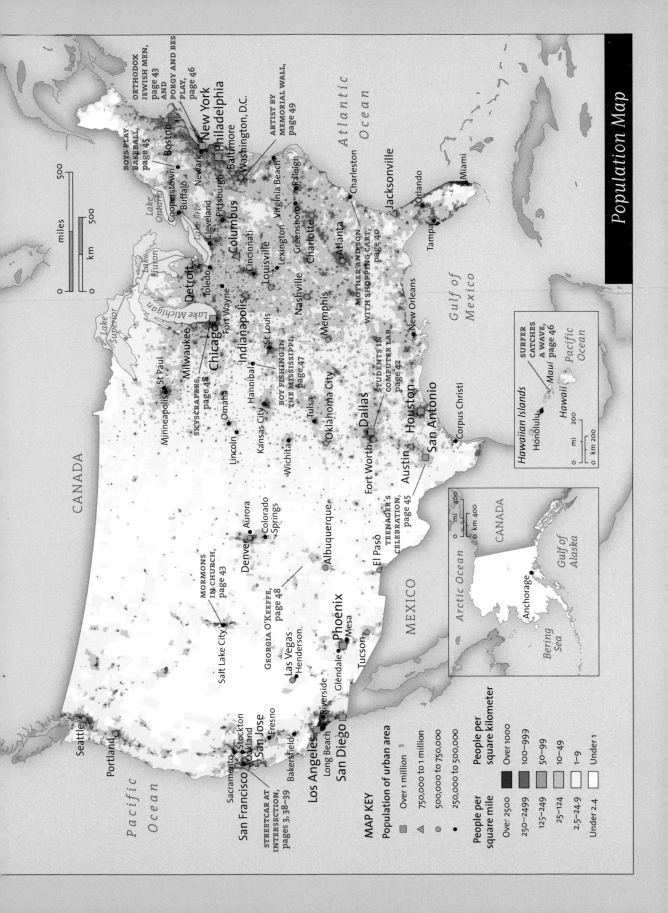

# Population Map

CANADA

## Pacific Ocean

Seattle
Portland

Sacramento
San Francisco

**STREETCAR AT INTERSECTION,**
pages 3, 38–39

Oakland
San Jose
Stockton
Fresno

Bakersfield

Los Angeles
Long Beach
Riverside
San Diego

**GEORGIA O'KEEFFE,**
page 48

Las Vegas
Henderson

Glendale
Phoenix
Mesa

Tucson

**MORMONS
IN CHURCH,**
page 43

Salt Lake City

Denver
Aurora
Colorado
Springs

Albuquerque

El Paso

CANADA

Anchorage

Arctic Ocean

MEXICO

*Gulf of
Alaska*

*Bering
Sea*

0        mi        400
0   km   400

Minneapolis
St Paul

**SKYSCRAPERS,**
page 48

Milwaukee
Chicago
Detroit
Toledo
Fort Wayne

Indianapolis

Lincoln
Omaha

Kansas City

St Louis

Hannibal

**BOY FISHING IN
THE MISSISSIPPI,**
page 47

Wichita

Tulsa

Oklahoma City

Fort Worth
Dallas

**MOTHER AND SON
WITH SHOPPING CART,**
page 40

**STUDENTS IN
COMPUTER LAB,**
page 42

Austin
Houston

**TEENAGER'S
CELEBRATION,**
page 45

San Antonio

Corpus Christi

Columbus
Cincinnati
Louisville
Lexington

Nashville
Memphis

New Orleans

MEXICO

*Gulf of
Mexico*

Cleveland
Pittsburgh

Columbus

Greensboro
Charlotte
Atlanta

Raleigh

Charleston

Jacksonville

Orlando

Tampa

Miami

**BOYS PLAY
BASEBALL,** page 45

Cooperstown
Buffalo

Boston

Newark
New York
Philadelphia
Baltimore
Washington, D.C.

Virginia Beach

**ORTHODOX
JEWISH MEN,**
page 43
**AND
PORGY AND BES**
PLAY,
page 46

**ARTIST BY
MEMORIAL WALL,**
page 49

*Atlantic
Ocean*

Lake Ontario
Lake Erie
Lake Huron
Lake Michigan
Lake Superior

*Hawaiian Islands*

Honolulu

Maui

**SURFER
CATCHES
A WAVE,**
page 46

Hawaii

*Pacific
Ocean*

0        mi        200
0   km   200

miles    500
km    500

0        0

## MAP KEY

### Population of urban area

▪ Over 1 million

▲ 750,000 to 1 million

● 500,000 to 750,000

• 250,000 to 500,000

### People per
square mile

### People per
square kilometer

| | |
|---|---|
| Over 2500 | Over 1000 |
| 250–2499 | 100–999 |
| 125–249 | 50–99 |
| 25–124 | 10–49 |
| 2.5–24.9 | 1–9 |
| Under 2.4 | Under 1 |

## Getting an Education

Most children in the United States must go to school from age 6 to 18. In some states, children may start school younger than this.

Students generally go to three schools: elementary school until they are 11, junior high from 11 to 14, and high school until they are 18. Public schools are free, but about 10 percent of parents pay to have their children attend private schools. About 3 percent of U.S. children—1.5 million kids—are taught at home.

A quarter of American adults have been to college after school and have at least a bachelor's degree. To go to college, students need good grades. They also have to pay tuition, which can be very high. Some students cannot afford a college education.

▲ Middle school students work in the computer lab at a school in Dallas, Texas.

## Religious Differences

Ever since the Pilgrims sailed from Europe, hundreds of thousands of people have come to America to be able to practice their faith freely. Today, the United States is one of the world's most religiously diverse countries. Just over half of Americans describe themselves as Protestants, while about one-quarter are Roman Catholic. Mormons make up just less

## AN AMERICAN RELIGION

The Church of the Latter Day Saints, or the Mormon Church, is known around the world. The church is based on Christianity but also follows the teachings of U.S. prophets—the "latter day saints." The religion was founded in the 1830s. Led by Brigham Young, the Mormons later moved to Utah, where the church still has its headquarters in Salt Lake City. The Mormons' unusual beliefs have brought them into conflict with the government. In the late 1850s, they even fought a short war with the U.S. Army for control of land in Utah. The most controversial Mormon practice is polygamy, in which a man may have several wives. This is against federal law. Today most Mormons reject polygamy.

▲ Worshippers crowd into the Mormon Tabernacle in Salt Lake City, Utah.

than 2 percent of the population. About 1.7 percent of Americans are Jewish, and 0.6 percent are Muslim.

## *World Cuisine*

It is difficult to describe typical American food because of the ethnic diversity of the country. You might think of hamburger and fries as a typical U.S. meal. In fact, the hamburger has its origins in Europe, just like other "American" dishes like pizza and hot dogs. One food that did originate in the United States is the favorite movie snack, popcorn. Native Americans showed European settlers how to make it, and it has been popular ever since.

▼ Two orthodox Jewish men have a snack in a deli in Brooklyn, New York. The United States is home to about 40 percent of the world's Jews.

▲ Two American inventions come together in theaters—popcorn and movies.

## Different Goals

Americans have sporting traditions that are often different from the sports enjoyed elsewhere around the world. The most popular U.S. sports are often minority sports in other countries. The most watched sport in America is football (known as gridiron in other countries) followed by baseball, basketball, and NASCAR racing. The world's most popular spectator sport, soccer, does not attract many U.S. television viewers. However, it is a very popular sport among pre-teenaged children. The U.S. women's soccer team is the most successful women's team in the world.

American football grew out of a game similar to rugby played in U.S. and Canadian colleges in the 1870s. Baseball was adapted from a British game called "rounders." However, basketball is an entirely American game, first played in New England in 1891. Another sport with its roots firmly in North

## NATIONAL HOLIDAYS

The holidays in the United States commemorate important moments in history and people that made the nation great.

| | |
|---|---|
| JAN 1 | New Year's Day |
| 3RD MONDAY, JAN | Martin Luther King, Jr., Day |
| 3RD MONDAY, FEB | Presidents' Day |
| MARCH OR APRIL | Easter Sunday |
| 4TH MONDAY, MAY | Memorial Day |
| JULY 4 | Independence Day |
| 1ST MONDAY, SEPT | Labor Day |
| 2ND MONDAY, OCT | Columbus Day |
| NOVEMBER 11 | Veterans' Day |
| 4TH THURSDAY, NOV | Thanksgiving |
| DECEMBER 25 | Christmas Day |

# HISPANIC AMERICANS

Before California and the Southwest became part of the United States, the region belonged to Mexico, and Hispanic culture is still strong there. In many ways, it has become part of everyday U.S. life. For example, the burritos and tacos of Tex-Mex food are a combination of Mexican and American food. In 2005, 14 percent of Americans were Hispanic. It is the fastest growing part of the U.S. population, and many Hispanic traditions are still practiced—but often with a U.S. flavor. One such tradition is the *Quince Años*, held on a girl's 15th birthday. The girl, or quinceañera, wears a white dress and celebrates becoming an adult.

▲ During her party, a quinceañera performs a dance with 14 of her friends.

America is ice hockey, which was played by Native Americans in the 17th century on frozen lakes. Traditionally, ice hockey, is most popular in colder states, where icy weather in more common. However, modern league hockey teams play all year around in indoor rinks. There is even a professional team in Tampa, Florida, where the outside temperature almost never falls below freezing.

Another traditional American sport is lacrosse. It is a little like hockey played in the air. Players use sticks with small nets on the end to pass around a small ball and score goals. Not many people play lacrosse today, but it has ancient roots. Native Americans were already playing a form of lacrosse when Europeans arrived in North America.

▼ A little league team plays at Doubleday Field in Cooperstown, New York. Legend has it that Abner Doubleday set out the rules to baseball on this site in 1839. However, different forms of the game were being played in America long before that date.

## SURF'S UP

**S**urfing is a growing sport around the world. Making surfboards and clothing is now a multi-billion dollar business. It all started over 200 years ago in Hawaii when the British explorer James Cook became the first European to visit the islands in 1778. Locals taught him to surf! Hawaiians surfed naked— but Cook kept his clothes on.

Pacific Islanders surfed on boards carved from trees. Some communities even used surf competitions to choose their chiefs. Today enthusiasts travel the world to ride the biggest waves they can find. California and Australia are major surfing areas, but Hawaii is still the world's surf capital. The old long, heavy wooden boards have been replaced by plastic "shortboards" that allow surfers to do more tricks.

▲ Modern surfers use shortboards because they are easier to steer and perform tricks.

▼ *Porgy and Bess* by George Gershwin has only African-American characters, which caused controversy when it was written in 1935.

# Musical Styles

One of America's biggest cultural influences in the 20th century was its many styles of music. Jazz started in New Orleans where it was influenced by the music of the Creoles, a community descended from Spanish, French, and African people. Jazz spread to New York and Chicago in the 1920s It was popularized by musicians such as Louis Armstrong and, later, Miles Davis. Blues and gospel evolved from the music of African slaves working in the

South. Along with jazz, they laid the foundation for the later forms of music, such as rock 'n' roll and hip hop.

In the 1950s, American musicians such as Elvis Presley became the first global pop stars. Later artists, such as Michael Jackson, Madonna, and Bruce Springsteen, have helped American music stay at the top of the pop charts for more than 50 years.

## Land of Writers

In the 19th century, poets Emily Dickinson and Walt Whitman wrote about daily life, while Herman Melville described the New England whaling industry in his novel *Moby Dick* (1851). Harriet Beecher Stowe wrote *Uncle Tom's Cabin* (1852) to protest slavery. It is said that when the Civil War began, Abraham Lincoln called her "the little lady who wrote the book that started this great war." *The Adventures of Huckleberry Finn*, by Mark Twain, appeared in 1884. Its heroes, Tom Sawyer and Huck Finn, are still among the most popular characters in U.S. literature. In the 20th century novelists such as Ernest Hemingway, William Faulkner, and F. Scott Fitzgerald considered what it meant to be an

▲ Every year Hannibal, Missouri, holds Tom Sawyer Day. The town, on the banks of the Mississippi River, was the childhood home of Mark Twain, and the residents remember him by dressing up as characters from his most famous book.

American. The plays of Eugene O'Neill and Tennessee Williams explored the hardships of American life. Popular children's books included Doctor Seuss's *Cat in the Hat* series and E.B. White's *Charlotte's Web*.

## Crafting Art

▲ Georgia O'Keeffe did most of her work in the Ghost Ranch area of New Mexico where she lived for almost 50 years. The artist is seen here beside the painting "Black Place III."

▶ Chicago is the home of the skyscraper. The city's Willis Tower, formerly known as the Sears Tower, is the tallest building in the United States.

Many of the world's greatest painters and architects have been American. Modern art bloomed in the country during the 20th century. The abstract artist Jackson Pollock made splatter paintings in the 1950s. In the 1960s Andy Warhol was a leader of the Pop Art movement, which tried to make art out of everyday

## MAYA'S MOVING SCAR

Completely unknown before 1981, Maya Lin was the surprise winner of a competition to design a memorial for those who died in the Vietnam War. Lin's winning design was very simple. It resembled a scar dug into the earth, with two wedge-shaped black walls set at an angle. Carved into the walls are the names of the 58,253 Americans, arranged in the order in which they died. The memorial was built in Washington, D.C., and soon proved very popular. Veterans and people who lost friends or family in the war find it very moving to seek out and touch the names of the dead.

Maya Lin went on to work as an artist as well as an architect. The two roles are often entwined in her work. Her most recent building, the Museum of Chinese America (MOCA), opened in New York City in 2009.

▲ Maya Lin stands beside the Vietnam Memorial when it was completed in 1982. Lin was born in Ohio. Her parents came from China in 1949.

objects. More traditional painting was given a new perspective by Edward Hopper, who captured urban life, and Georgia O'Keefe, who focused on the beauty of the desert.

By the early 20th century a distinctive American style of architecture had developed: skyscrapers. The first skyscrapers—steel-framed buildings with dozens of floors—were built in Chicago and then New York City. Today, they are seen in all large cities.

Since the 1920s, Los Angeles, California, has been the hub of the movie industry. Because of this people around the world are often more familiar with how Americans live than they are with the cultures of nearer countries. But their image of America comes from Hollywood movies and U.S. television shows—it doesn't always reflect reality.

# In Pursuit
## of
# Happiness

**T**HE GLEAMING WHITE DOME of the Capitol Building shines in the sun. The Capitol Building is the most important building in the U.S. capital, Washington D.C. Its position at the top of Capitol Hill—known in Washington simply as the Hill—reflects its significance as the seat of the federal government. It is here that the most important decisions are made, the laws that apply to all 50 U.S. states. Located on the far side of the Hill, the Supreme Court is the only other institution that can change U.S. laws.

If you stand on the steps in front of the Capitol Building, all the other buildings that line the Hill appear much smaller, including the White House where the President lives. Congress has passed a law to prevent any buildings in the city from being taller than the dome of the Capitol Building.

◀ **Today's Capitol building was constructed in 1868.**

# ONE COUNTRY, FIFTY STATES

The United States is divided into 50 states. The states vary in size from tiny Rhode Island to the vast state of Alaska. Some of the states, particularly those on the eastern seaboard such as New York and New Jersey, are densely populated while western states like Montana are far less crowded. California has the most people with more than 36 million inhabitants, and Wyoming is the least populated with just over 500,000 residents. Washington, D.C., the U.S. capital city, is not in any state, but forms the self-governing District of Columbia. Territories such as Puerto Rico in the Caribbean and Guam in the Pacific are not states but are still represented in the U.S. Congress.

## Trading Partners

The United States has the world's largest economy. The economies of many countries rely on selling products, such as cars, cell phones, or oil, to the United States. When Americans buy these products, the effects are felt around the world. One saying puts it this way: "When the United States sneezes, the rest of the world catches a cold."

| Country | Percent United States exports |
|---|---|
| Canada | 21.4% |
| Mexico | 11.7% |
| China | 5.6% |
| Japan | 5.4% |
| All others combined | 54.9% |

| Country | Percent United States imports |
|---|---|
| China | 16.9% |
| Canada | 15.7% |
| Mexico | 10.6% |
| Japan | 7.4% |
| All others combined | 49.4% |

▼ Atlantic City is one of the many urban areas in New Jersey—the most crowded U.S. state.

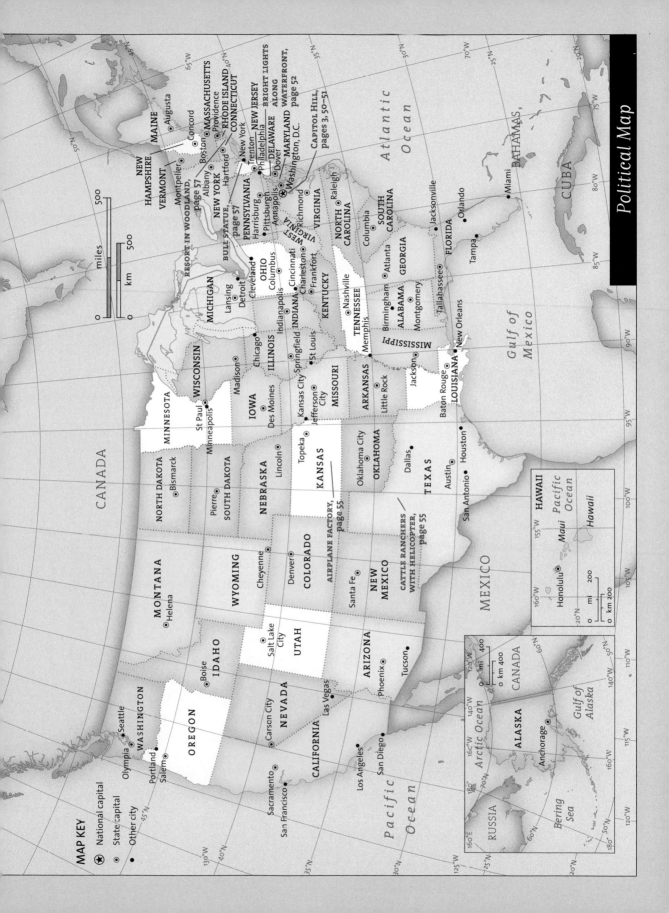

Political Map

# For the People, by the People

Since the United States declared independence in 1776, Americans have been figuring out how to govern themselves. Although the federal government passes the laws of the country, each state can also make its own laws. The Founders who wrote the Constitution in 1787 set out to balance federal and state power. They also divided the federal government in three. The executive, legislative, and judicial branches each have specific roles that stop the other branches from having too much power. They operate a system of what are known as "checks and balances."

## HOW THE GOVERNMENT WORKS

The United States is a republic. The head of state is a President, who is elected every four years. Laws are passed by the U.S. Congress. This has two houses, the Senate and the House of Representatives. The Senate has 100 members, with two members elected by popular vote from each state every six years. There are 435 Representatives in the House. Each one represents a region that is home to a similar number of people. Representatives are elected for two-year terms. The U.S. President is elected by an electoral college. After the people have voted, each state sends a certain number of delegates to Washington to vote for the president. States with large populations send more delegates. The highest U.S. court is the Supreme Court. Its judges are appointed by the President and serve for life—or until they choose to retire.

| GOVERNMENT | | |
|---|---|---|
| EXECUTIVE | LEGISLATIVE | JUDICIARY |
| PRESIDENT | SENATE (100 MEMBERS) | SUPREME COURT |
| DEPARTMENTS AND AGENCIES | HOUSE OF REPRESENTATIVES (435 MEMBERS) | CIRCUIT COURTS OF APPEAL |

Each state has a governor, which is its highest political office. The governor runs the state government, which is responsible for things such as police, schools, and highway maintenance. The governor's work is overseen by state representatives who serve in the state legislature.

Two political parties have dominated U.S. politics since the 1790s: the Democrats and the Republicans. Members of Congress are elected at different times from the President, so it has often happened that the President is from one party while Congress is controlled by the other. Again, this helps prevent either party from becoming too powerful.

## Working the Land

A hundred years ago, the United States was an agricultural country where most people worked on the land. Today, two-fifths of the land is used for farming, but less than 1 percent of the labor force are farmers. Much of their work has been mechanized. The United States is the world's greatest producer of agricultural commodities, such as wheat and corn. The huge prairies are ideal farmland, and irrigation systems have converted

▲ The United States is the largest producer of aircraft. This airliner is being constructed at a Boeing factory in Wichita, Kansas.

▼ The cattle ranches in Texas are enormous. This one is so large that ranchers use a helicopter to round up herds with help from traditional cowboys on horseback.

# INDUSTRY AND AGRICULTURE

The United States is very rich in minerals and other natural resources, such as lumber. It also has a huge expanse of agricultural land, much of which is irrigated to increase fertility. This map shows where major industries are located around the country.

**MAP KEY**

- ✿ Manufacturing center
- Al Processing plant
- Steel Steel manufacturing
- ⛏ Coal
- 🛢 Petroleum

**Major Mines**
- **Al** Aluminum
- **Cu** Copper
- **Au** Gold
- **Fe** Iron
- **Pb** Lead
- **Ag** Silver
- **Zn** Zinc

Seattle
Portland
Zn
Pb Ag
Rocky Mountains
Fe
Fe
Minneapolis
Milwaukee
Chicago
Detroit
Steel
Steel
Steel
Pittsburgh
Boston
New York
Philadelphia
Baltimore
Denver
Au
Au
Ag
Cu
Ag
Au
Au
Zn
Pb
Al
Charlotte
Los Angeles
Au Cu
Atlanta
Dallas
Houston
Al
*Pacific Ocean*
*Atlantic Ocean*
*Gulf of Mexico*

0  400 mi
0  400 km

Zn
Pb Ag
Au

*Bering Sea*
*Gulf of Alaska*

0   mi   500
0   km  500

the drier plains and desert regions into fertile farmland. Livestock is also a vital part of farming. It earns around half of the country's total agricultural income of $240 billion each year.

## Changing Times

Much of the wealth of the United States came from its manufacturing industry. Since the late 19th century, mechanized factories and inexpensive labor meant that Americans could make anything they needed and sell the surplus abroad. However, the last 20 years have brought a shift in production away from the United States to countries such as China, where the costs of manufacturing are now much lower.

The United States continues to excel in high-tech manufacturing, such as building airplanes, but today most Americans work in the service industry. They use their skills and knowledge not to make things but to provide services. Large service industries include healthcare, education, and tourism. Another powerful

# CASINO COUNTERCULTURE

In the 19th century, most Native American groups were forced onto reservations, often on poor land. Each tribe has political control over its land, however, and today many have discovered a new way to earn money: casinos. Casinos are legal in a few cities in Nevada and in Atlantic City, New Jersey—but nowhere else. All the others are on tribal lands. Along with mining rights, which tribes also control, casinos are an important source of income for groups who have traditionally found it hard to get work. The largest casino in the United States is run by the Mashantucket Pequot people of Connecticut. It has 380 gaming tables. If one person from the reservation sat at each table, about 60 tables would be left empty—the entire Mashantucket Pequot nation numbers only about 320 people.

▲ As well as casinos, the Mashantucket complex has a museum and research center.

and important service industry is finance and banking. Wall Street in New York City is a tiny street, but it lies at the heart of the world economy. It is home to the New York Stock Exchange.

## *The Future*

Since 1945, the United States has been the leading economic power in the world. Today, it faces a steep drop in wealth that has not been seen since the 1930s. Will the United States retain its strong global position? No one knows, but one thing seems certain: Americans will continue to be known for their positive outlook and their refusal to be beaten. The American dream of building a better life is sure to survive.

▼ A bronze bull stands in Bowling Green, a small park in the heart of New York's Financial District and a short walk from Wall Street. The bull represents the strength and optimism of the U.S. financial industry.

# Add a Little Extra to Your Country Report!

I f you are assigned to write a report about the United States, you'll want to include basic information about the country, of course. The Fast Facts chart on page 8 will give you a good start. The rest of the book will give you the details you need to create a full and up-to-date paper or PowerPoint presentation. But what can you do to make your report more fun than anyone else's? If you use your imagination and dig a bit deeper into some of the topics introduced in this book, you're sure to come up with information that will make your report unique!

## >Flag

Perhaps you could explain the history of the flag of the United States and the meanings of its colors and symbols. Go to **www.crwflags.com/fotw/flags** for more information.

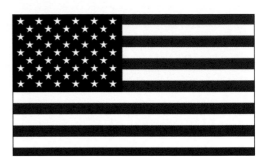

## >National Anthem

How about downloading the U.S. national anthem and playing it for your class? At **www.nationalanthems.info** you'll find what you need, including sheet music for it. Simply pick "U" and then "United States" from the list on the left-hand side of the screen, and you're on your way.

## >Time Difference

If you want to understand the time difference between the United States and where you are, this Web site can help: **www.worldtimeserver.com**. Just pick "United States" from the list on the left. If you called someone in the United States right now, would you wake them up from their sleep? Keep in mind that there are six time zones in the United States.

## >Currency

Another Web site will convert your money into dollars, the currency used in the United States. You'll want to know how much money to bring if you travel to the United States: **www.xe.com/ucc**.

## >Weather

Why not check the current weather in United States? It's easy—go to **www.weather.com** to find out if it's sunny or cloudy, warm, or cold in the United States right now! The country is so large that the weather in one region can be completely different from the condition in another. Click on several cities in turn to get a full picture of the U.S. weather. Be sure to click on the tabs below the weather report for Sunrise/Sunset information, Weather Watch, and Business Travel Outlook, too. Scroll down the page for the 36-Hour Forecast and a satellite weather map. Compare your weather to the weather in the U.S. cities you chose. Is this a good season for a person to travel around the United States?

## >Miscellaneous

Still want more information? Simply go to National Geographic's World Atlas for Young Explorers at **http://www.nationalgeographic.com/ kids-world-atlas**. It will help you find maps, photos, music, games, and other features that you can use to jazz up your report.

# Glossary

**Architecture**  the practice of making buildings.

**Butte**  a flat-topped hill.

**Civil war**  when two or more groups living in the same country fight each other for control of all or part of the territory.

**Climate**  the average weather of a certain place at different times of the year.

**Colony**  a region that is ruled by a nation located somewhere else in the world. Settlers from that distant country take the land from the region's original inhabitants.

**Culture**  a collection of beliefs, traditions, and styles that belongs to people living in a certain part of the world.

**Delta**  a system of mudbanks and channels that forms when a river splits into several streams before reaching the sea.

**Democracy**  a country that is ruled by a government chosen by its people using elections.

**Economy**  the system by which a country creates wealth through trading products.

**Empire**  territories located in several parts of the world that are controlled by a single nation.

**Endangered**  at risk of dying out.

**Estuary**  river mouth.

**Exported**  transported and sold abroad.

**Gold Rush**  a period when people move to an area in the hope of finding gold and becoming rich overnight. There was a gold rush in California in 1848.

**Great Depression**  a period in the 1930s when the United States and much of the world became poorer.

**Habitat**  a part of the environment that is suitable for certain plants and animals.

**Herbivore**  an animal that eats only plants.

**Hunter-gatherers**  members of a primitive culture that do not produce food using farming. Instead, people gather plants and hunt animals.

**Imported**  brought into the country from abroad.

**Midwest**  an area of the United States that stretches from the Great Lakes across the Upper Mississippi Valley.

**Militia**  a military force made up of civilian volunteers. Modern militias are generally called out in emergency situations. In U.S. history, the militias serving early American colonies formed the basis of the revolutionary army.

**Patriot**  a person who supports his or her country. American colonists who rebelled against British rule were called patriots. Those who chose to stay British were known as loyalists.

**Peninsula**  a region of land that is surrounded by water on three sides and attached to a mainland by a narrow strip of land.

**Republic**  a country that has an elected president as its head of state.

**Superpower**  a very powerful and wealthy country that has a lot of influence over a large group of less powerful allies and so has interests in all parts of the world. The United States has been regarded as a superpower since the 1940s.

# Bibliography

Jones, J. *Created Equal: A Social and Political History of the United States.* New York: Pearson Longman, 2008.

Lewis, Michael. *American Wilderness: A New History.* Oxford: Oxford University

Press, 2007.

Nash, Gary B. *Atlas of American History.* New York: Facts on File, 2007.

http://www.census.gov/ (United States Census Bureau)

http://www.america.gov/ (general information)

http://news.bbc.co.uk/1/hi/ world/americas/country_ profiles/1217752.stm (general information)

# Further Information

## NATIONAL GEOGRAPHIC Articles

"America Then and Now." NATIONAL GEOGRAPHIC TRAVELER (January/February 2009): 45–69.

## Web sites to explore

More fast facts about the United States, from the CIA (Central Intelligence Agency): https://www.cia.gov/library/ publications/the-world-factbook/geos/us.html

The United States is full of amazing sights. This Web site gives you a great view of many of them using 360° panoramas. This link takes you on a flight over Las Vegas, Nevada—check out the embedded views—but there are hundreds of other scenes. Take a look: http://bigeyein thesky.com/View.asp?ID=709 &CID=Las_Vegas

New York City's Museum of Modern Art, or MoMA, has one of the greatest collections of paintings, sculptures, and other forms of art from the 20th century. You can browse through it all using this link. http://www.moma.org/explore/ collection/

Ever wondered how Americans ended up speaking like they do? Perhaps a good place to begin finding out is to listen to how the first pilgrims spoke to each other. This site lets you do just that, and a whole lot more: http://www.plimoth.org/ kids/talk.php

One of the most unusual and rare animals in North America is the manatee. Take a closer look at these amazing animals in the wild at http://www.savethemanatee. org/video.htm

## See, hear

There are many ways to get a taste of life in the United States, such as movies and music. Here are two suggestions:

*Cajun music and zydeco*
These two lesser known styles of American music come from the centuries-old French and African communities of Louisiana and Texas. Search for music of this type on an online mp3 store.

*Grapes of Wrath*
This novel by John Steinbeck was published in 1939 as the Great Depression drew to a close. It tells the story of an American family's struggle to make ends meet during the Depression and is considered one of the best novels ever written, in any language.

# Index

Boldface indicates illustrations.

# Credits

## Picture Credits

Front Cover – Spine: istockphoto: Top: Ned Frisk/Blend Images/Getty Images; Low Far Left: Michael S. Yamishita/NGIC; Low Left: Roy Toft/ NGIC; Low Right: William Albert Allard/NGIC; Low Far Right: Ralph Lee Hopkins/NGIC.

Interior – Corbis: Bob Daemmrich: 42 up; Patrick Giardino: TP; Philip Gould: 12 up; Catherine Karnow: 43 lo; Layne Kennedy: 22 up; Bob krist: 2-3, 26-27; Owaki Kulla: 11 lo; Buddy Mays: 47 up; PictureNet: 52 lo; Jose Fuste Raga: 2 left, 5 up, 6-7; Galen Rowell: 18 lo; Peter Ulrich/epa: 46 lo; istockphoto: 59; NGIC: William Albert Allard: 3 left, 38-39, 55 lo; James L. Amos: 35 lo; Annie Griffiths Belt: 24 up; Peter V. Bianchi: 28 right; James P. Blair: 36 up, 43 up, 49 up; Jonathan Blair: 32 lo; Ira Block: 55 up; Peter Carsten: 13 lo; David Edwards: 14 up; Raymond Gehman: 15 up, 30 lo; Stacy Gold: 10 left; Justin Guariglia: 57 lo; Nadia M.B. Hughes: 48 lo; Otis Imboden: Chris Johns: 22 lo; 11 up; Tim Laman: 21 up; Sarah Leen: 40 lo; Luis Marden: 32 up; Patrick McFeeley: 46 up; George Mobley: 33 up, 48 up; Robert W. Moore: 23 lo; NASA: 37 up; Klaus Nigge: 2 right, 16-17; Steve Raymer: 14 lo; Pete Ryan: 34 lo; Steven St John: 45 lo; Joe Satore: 24 lo, 25 up; Phil Schemeister: 31 lo; Richard Schlecht: 30 up; Joe Stancampiano: 20up; Maggie Steber: 35 up, 57 up; Rex A Stucky: 3 right, 50-51; Paul Sutherland: 21 lo; Medford Taylor: 34 up; Steve Winter: 37 lo.

For more information, please call 1-800-NGS-LINE (647-5463) or write to the following address:

NATIONAL GEOGRAPHIC SOCIETY
1145 17th Street N.W.
Washington, D.C. 20036-4688 U.S.A.

Visit us online at www.nationalgeographic.com/books

Library of Congress Cataloging-in-Publication Data available on request
ISBN: 978-1-4263-0632-7

Printed in the United States of America

Series design by Jim Hiscott.
The body text is set in Avenir; Knockout.
The display text is set in Matrix Script.

Front Cover—Top: Girl running with American flag on farm; Low Far Left: Chrysler Building, New York City; Low Left: Bald eagle; Low Right: Minor league batting practice, Reno, Nevada; Low Far Right: Rainbow, Grand Canyon.

Page 1—Little League baseball players; Icon image on spine, Contents page, and throughout: Detail of Navajo weaving

## Produced through the worldwide resources of the National Geographic Society

John M. Fahey, Jr., *President and Chief Executive Officer*; Gilbert M. Grosvenor, *Chairman of the Board*; Tim T. Kelly, *President, Global Media Group*; John Q. Griffin, *President, Publishing*; Nina D. Hoffman, *Executive Vice President, President of Book Publishing Group*; Melina Gerosa Bellows, *Executive Vice President, Children's Publishing*

## National Geographic Staff for this Book

Nancy Laties Feresten, *Vice President, Editor-in-Chief of Children's Books*
Jonathan Halling, *Design Director*
Jim Hiscott, *Art Director*
Rebecca Baines, *Project Editor*
Lori Epstein, *Illustrations Editor*
Grace Hill, *Associate Managing Editor*
Stacy Gold, Nadia Hughes, *Illustrations Research Editors*
R. Gary Colbert, *Production Director*
Lewis R. Bassford, *Production Manager*
Nicole Elliott, *Manufacturing Manager*
Maps, *Mapping Specialists, Ltd.*

## Brown Reference Group plc. Staff for this Book

*Volume Editor: Tom Jackson*
*Designer: Dave Allen*
*Picture Manager: Sophie Mortimer*
*Maps: Martin Darlison*
*Artwork: Darren Awuah*
*Senior Managing Editor: Tim Cooke*
*Children's Publisher: Anne O'Daly*
*Editorial Director: Lindsey Lowe*

## About the Author

ELDEN CROY was born in Kansas and raised in Kansas, Texas, and Colorado, where he graduated from the University of Colorado at Boulder. He studied as an architect at the Architectural Association in London, England, where he now lives. He returns frequently to the United States to visit his family, who are widely scattered among the states.

## About the Consultants

JOHN FRASER HART is a professor of geography at the University of Minnesota in Minneapolis. His research has focused on the geography of rural areas in the United States, on which he has published a number of books and articles. He is a former President of the Association of American Geographers, and was the recipient of the Vouras Medal from the American Geographical Society for his contributions to regional geography.

CATHERINE GUDIS is a professor of U.S. history at the University of California, Riverside. Her research and teaching interests are in the fields of consumer and visual culture, the built environment, and public history. Professor Gudis is the author of *Buyways: Billboards, Automobiles, and the American Landscape* and a coeditor of *Cultures of Commerce: Representations of Business Culture in the United States*. She has also worked for many years in museums and historic preservation organizations.

09/WOR/1

# Time Line of U.S. History

## 1500

**1550** The Cayuga, Mohawk, Oneida, and Onondaga form the League of the Iroquois to stop conflict among them.

**1565** The Spanish found St. Augustine in Florida, the first permanent European settlement in North America.

## 1600

**1620** English Puritans, known as the Pilgrims, establish Plymouth Colony, near Cape Cod. The settlement encourages other colonists to emigrate to the northeast.

## 1700

**1754** The French and Indian War begins between England and France. The 1763 Treaty of Paris ends the war and gives England control of all territory east of the Mississippi River.

**1773** New England colonial merchants protest a British tax on tea by throwing valuable tea into Boston harbor.

**1774** Colonial representatives meet at the First Continental Congress to discuss independence. King George III sends troops to Massachusetts.

**1776** On July 4, Independence Day, the Continental Congress approves the Declaration of Independence.

**1783** The Treaty of Paris ends the war and recognizes the United States.

**1787** Delegates from the thirteen states meet in Philadelphia to draft a constitution. A year later, the constitution is approved and the three branches of government are established.

**1791** Ten amendments are made to the Constitution; they are collectively known as the Bill of Rights.

## 1800

**1803** The Louisiana Purchase of land from France doubles the size of the United States.

**1812** The United States declares war on England over restrictions on U.S. trade. The war lasts three years and inspires Francis Scott Key to write the national anthem, "The Star-Spangled Banner."

**1820** The Missouri Compromise keeps the number of northern free states and southern slave states equal in the U.S. Senate as the nation expands west.

**1830** Congress passes the Indian Removal Act, which allows southeastern states to force American Indians such as the Cherokee, Creek, Choctaw, Chickasaw, and Seminole to move west of the Mississippi.

**1848** The United States wins the Mexican War and gains present-day Texas, New Mexico, and much of California.

**1861** The Civil War begins between the Confederate States of America, led by Jefferson Davis, and the Union, led by President Abraham Lincoln. The war costs 600,000 lives.

**1865** The Union wins the war; Congress passes the Thirteenth Amendment, which abolishes slavery; President Lincoln is assassinated.

**1882** The Chinese Exclusion Act prohibits the continued immigration of Chinese laborers to the United States.